Early EXPLORERS

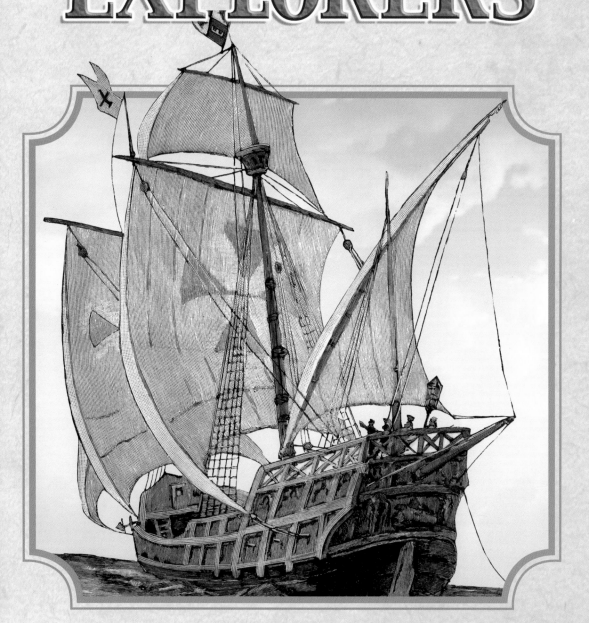

Heather E. Schwartz

Consultants

Katie Blomquist, M.Ed.
Fairfax County Public Schools

Nicholas Baker, Ed.D.
Supervisor of Curriculum and Instruction
Colonial School District, DE

Publishing Credits

Rachelle Cracchiolo, M.S.Ed., *Publisher*
Conni Medina, M.A.Ed., *Managing Editor*
Emily R. Smith, M.A.Ed., *Series Developer*
Diana Kenney, M.A.Ed., NBCT, *Content Director*
Johnson Nguyen, *Multimedia Designer*
Lynette Ordoñez, *Editor*

Image Credits: Cover, pp. 1, 2–3, 7, 12–13, 14 (ship), 15, 17, 18, 19, 21 North Wind Picture Archives; p. 5 and back cover LOC [g3200. mf000070]; pp. 4, 10, 20, 24–25, 26 Granger, NYC; p. 8 DeA Picture Library/The Granger Collection; p. 9 Gerry Embleton/North Wind Picture Archives; p. 11 DEA/J. E. BULLOZ/Getty Images; p. 12 De Agostini Picture Library/Bridgeman Images; p. 14 Classic Image/Alamy; p .15 From the National Library of Portugal (Biblioteca Nacional de Portugal); pp. 16–17 LOC [g3200.ct000725]; p. 19 Sémhur/Wikimedia Commons/CC-BY-SA-3.0; p. 21 LOC [ct000738]; p. 22 GL Archive/Alamy; p. 23 Mary Evans Picture Library/Alamy; p. 24 World History Archive/Alamy; p. 25 Mcapdevila/Wikimedia Commons/CC-BY-SA-3.0; pp. 26, 32 Wikimedia Commons/Public Domain; p. 27 LOC [LC-USZ62-76273]; all other images from iStock and/or Shutterstock.

Library of Congress Cataloging-in-Publication Data

Names: Schwartz, Heather E., author.
Title: Early explorers / Heather E. Schwartz.
Description: Huntington Beach, CA : Teacher Created Materials, 2016. |
  Includes index. | Audience: Grade 4 to 6.?
Identifiers: LCCN 2015051140 (print) | LCCN 2016012860 (ebook) | ISBN
  9781493830732 (pbk.) | ISBN 9781480756755 (eBook)
Subjects: LCSH: Discoveries in geography--Juvenile literature.
Classification: LCC G175 .S353 2016 (print) | LCC G175 (ebook) | DDC
  910.9--dc23
LC record available at http://lccn.loc.gov/2015051140

Teacher Created Materials
5301 Oceanus Drive
Huntington Beach, CA 92649-1030
http://www.tcmpub.com

ISBN 978-1-4938-3073-2

Table of Contents

World Travelers

Early explorers traveled the globe hundreds of years ago. When they set out on their journeys, they did not know much about the world. They did not have accurate maps to follow. And they didn't have today's technology to guide them. Their understanding of waterways and **continents** was limited. Still, they set out into the unknown.

Explorers left their homes in Europe, and brought back valuable information when they returned. Many of these explorers became famous for their findings. They were **credited** with discovering new areas of the world that no one from Europe had ever seen.

Christopher Columbus arrives in the Americas.

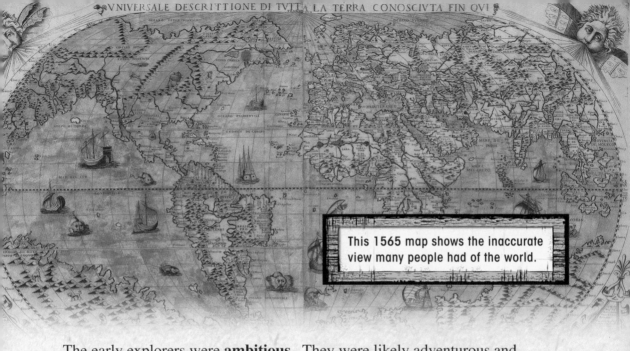

This 1565 map shows the inaccurate view many people had of the world.

The early explorers were **ambitious**. They were likely adventurous and courageous. The explorers could not predict the dangers they would encounter along the way. They didn't always arrive where they expected. And they did not know if they would ever return home. Yet many of them went on multiple **expeditions**. They set out again and again to see all they could and to make the unknown known. However, they often seemed to have little concern for the **native** people who lived in these new lands. Many explorers killed them, took what they wanted, and left.

Who were these early explorers? Why did they risk their lives to travel the world?

Discoveries Demystified

Early explorers found areas of the globe they had never seen. But other people had lived there for thousands of years. The explorers' findings are called *discoveries* because they discovered the land for Europe.

pyramids in Mexico

5

Medieval Exploration

The Vikings were some of the earliest explorers. They came from Scandinavia. Their homeland was too cold for year-round farming. So during the eighth century, they left home to find food. They sailed across the North Sea and landed in different parts of Europe. Vikings raided towns and claimed land as their own. They settled in Ireland, Scotland, and England. Later, they sailed the Atlantic Ocean. They explored and settled in Iceland and Greenland. These are islands between North America and Europe.

Scandinavia on the Map

Scandinavia is in northern Europe. It includes Norway, Sweden, Finland, Denmark, Iceland, and the Faroe Islands. About 25 percent of the region is north of the Arctic Circle.

Vikings traveled from Greenland to North America in the 11th century. They settled in Newfoundland, an island off the coast of Canada. They had landed over 1,000 miles from Greenland. The site is now called L'Anse aux (LANS OH) Meadows. It is the earliest known settlement of Europeans in North America.

By 1100, countries were getting better at defending themselves against Viking attacks. Vikings traded more and battled less. They also traveled less. They settled into their new homes, and some joined other European countries. They left their settlements in North America.

Bird Navigation

Vikings watched flying birds to predict where land might be located. They thought that birds with empty beaks were likely going out to sea to hunt. But birds with full beaks were most likely heading toward land.

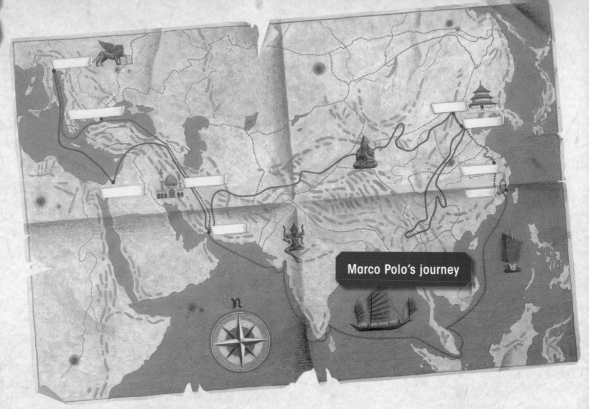

Marco Polo's journey

Exploration did not end with the Vikings. People from other European countries also wanted to leave home and see the world. Some wanted adventure. Many wanted to gain wealth. Others wanted to learn about different **cultures**.

Marco Polo grew up in Venice, Italy, during the 13th century. His father and uncles were explorers. For the first 15 years of Polo's life, his father and uncles were away. Among other places, they visited Cathay, now the country of Mongolia. They met Kublai Khan, Cathay's ruler. They came home and met Polo in 1269.

Silk Road

Despite how it sounds, the Silk Road was not just one road. It was many routes developed centuries earlier. It linked Europe and Asia for trade.

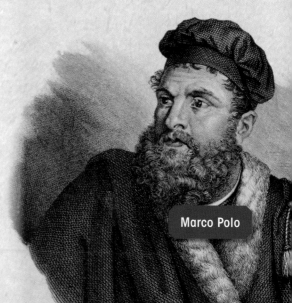

Marco Polo

In 1271, they set out to return to Cathay. This time, Polo went with them. He was about 17 years old. For three to four years, they traveled along the Silk Road. They went through deserts and mountain passes. At one point, Polo became very ill.

Finally, they reached their destination. Marco Polo joined Khan's court. He learned the Mongolian language and **customs**. He traveled farther into Asia for Khan. He visited Tibet, Burma, and India. Polo stayed with Khan for 17 years. He became very wealthy.

Polo returned to Europe after being gone for 24 years. He told of his adventures. These stories were written as a book. But it is not certain whether the author was Polo or an acquaintance. His story inspired others to travel and explore the world.

Polo plays chess with Kublai Khan.

Gaining Gunpowder

Gunpowder was a Chinese invention. It came to Europe in the 13th century through invasions and trade routes. Gunpowder made it easier for European explorers to claim land and to easily defeat people living there.

Age of Discovery

By the 15th century, the Silk Road was not a safe route for travel between Europe and Asia. War in China made it too dangerous. There were also thieves who attacked traders along the way. This change sparked a new beginning. It was the start of the Age of Discovery.

No one wanted to stop trading with Asia. Spices from Asia had many uses. They flavored foods and preserved meat. They were also used to preserve the dead as well as cure fevers and other health problems. But most spices didn't grow in the colder European climate.

This merchant sells spices and herbs from Asia in the 13th century.

Marco Polo visits pepper harvesters in southern India.

Europeans needed a safer way to get to Asia. They also needed a shorter route to make spices more affordable. Some spices cost as much as gold! Spices passed from trader to trader during the long journey across the Silk Road. Each trader raised the price. By the time they reached Europe, the spices were very expensive. Only very wealthy people could afford them. So Europeans focused on finding a safer, shorter water route between the continents.

In 1487, Bartolomeu Dias (bar-TAHL-uh-myoo DEE-uhs) left Portugal. He sailed around the southern tip of Africa. He found that the Atlantic Ocean and the Indian Ocean were connected. It was an exciting discovery. This meant there was a water route around Africa to Asia.

An Italian explorer felt there was a better way. Christopher Columbus believed he could avoid traveling all the way around Africa. He was convinced he could reach Asia by sailing west instead. But no one had ever done this. It was a risky idea.

Bartolomeu Dias

Columbus's ships

Columbus hoped to sail for Portugal. But the king rejected his plan. He tried Italy, but had no luck there either. Spain rejected him, too. Later, though, Spain agreed to **sponsor** his trip. This meant Spain would pay his expenses. Any land that was discovered would be claimed for Spain in return. In August of 1492, he set sail for Asia. Instead of going south, he headed west. He brought Marco Polo's book with him. It inspired him to travel.

In October, Columbus spotted land. He was sure he had reached Asia.

Christopher Columbus

Not Afraid

Some think that before Columbus made his famous voyage, people believed the world was flat. But this is not true. People knew the world was round since ancient times. Columbus was not afraid of falling off the edge of the Earth.

Columbus claimed territory for Spain in 1492. But it was not the territory he believed it to be. Columbus thought he found a passage west from Europe to Asia. Spain's rulers thought so, too. But he never landed in Asia. He landed in the Americas. It was the same continent the Vikings had visited. But people in Europe didn't realize this at the time. Columbus never knew what he found.

Columbus was the first European to explore the Americas since the Vikings. But there were already people living there. Since Columbus thought he landed in India, he called the people Indians. Today, they are known as American Indians. They had lived in the Americas for thousands of years.

Rulers in Spain and Portugal both wanted to trade in this new land. A **treaty** gave each country rights to trade. It let them trade in different parts of the Americas. Both countries began claiming more and more land. They built large **empires**. But in doing so, they pushed American Indians out of their homelands. Soon, other countries would do the same. This pattern continued for hundreds of years.

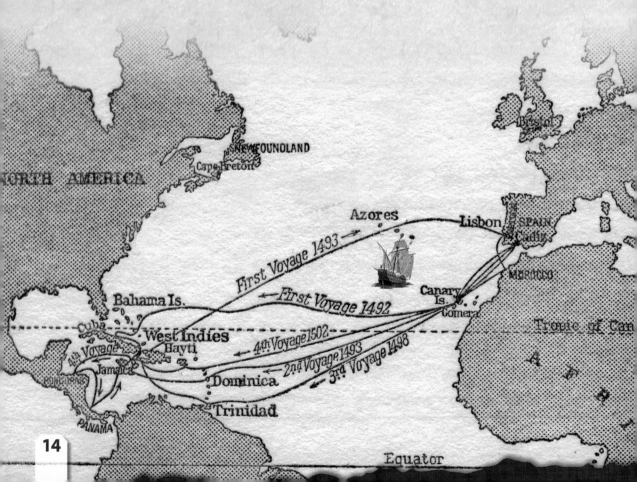

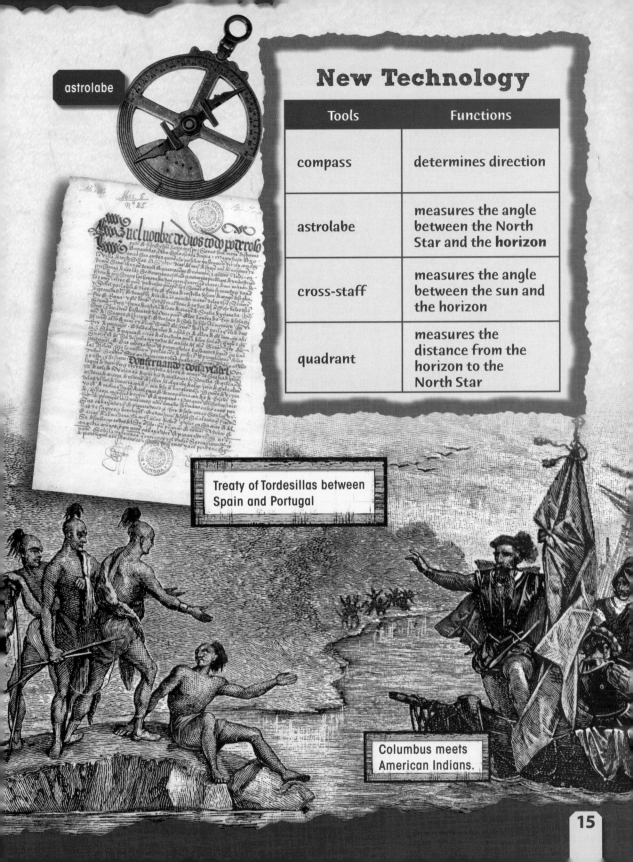

astrolabe

New Technology

Tools	Functions
compass	determines direction
astrolabe	measures the angle between the North Star and the **horizon**
cross-staff	measures the angle between the sun and the horizon
quadrant	measures the distance from the horizon to the North Star

Treaty of Tordesillas between Spain and Portugal

Columbus meets American Indians.

This 1507 map is the first to name the New World after Amerigo Vespucci.

Trial, Error, and Accomplishment

Spain's rulers expected plenty of gold and spices from India. And they wanted Columbus to bring these goods to them. Of course, he never made it to Asia. He found some gold and spices, but not the large amounts they wanted.

Over time, Spain's rulers began to doubt Columbus. Despite his claims, they did not believe he had landed in Asia. They sent more explorers. Amerigo Vespucci was one of them. He was Italian, but he first sailed for Spain. He later sailed for Portugal.

Gains and Losses

European explorers and American Indians engaged in trade. But the explorers did more than trade. They stole, spread diseases, and forced the American Indians to work for them. They claimed the land for their home countries.

Vespucci traveled to the land Columbus claimed was India. He returned home in 1502 and explained that it was an entirely new continent. He called it the New World.

In 1507, a German cartographer, or mapmaker, published a book. It featured information about the New World. He named a section of the New World for Vespucci. He called it America. Today, we know that the New World is actually two continents. Both North and South America still bear Amerigo Vespucci's name.

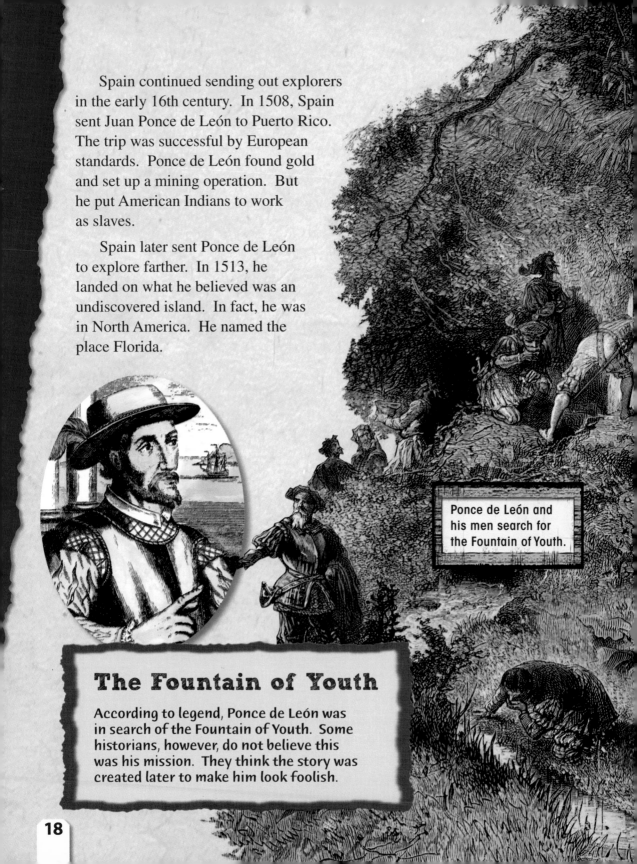

Spain continued sending out explorers in the early 16th century. In 1508, Spain sent Juan Ponce de León to Puerto Rico. The trip was successful by European standards. Ponce de León found gold and set up a mining operation. But he put American Indians to work as slaves.

Spain later sent Ponce de León to explore farther. In 1513, he landed on what he believed was an undiscovered island. In fact, he was in North America. He named the place Florida.

Ponce de León and his men search for the Fountain of Youth.

The Fountain of Youth

According to legend, Ponce de León was in search of the Fountain of Youth. Some historians, however, do not believe this was his mission. They think the story was created later to make him look foolish.

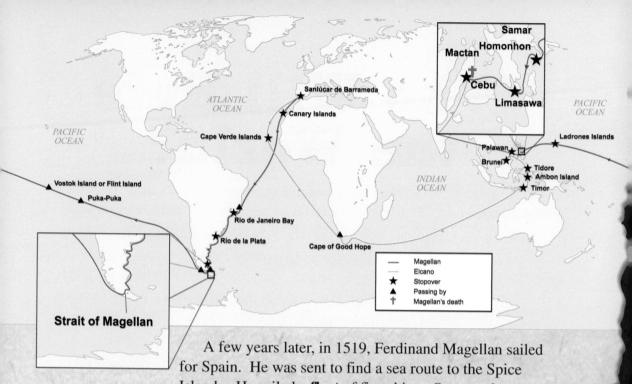

A few years later, in 1519, Ferdinand Magellan sailed for Spain. He was sent to find a sea route to the Spice Islands. He sailed a **fleet** of five ships. One was lost to storms. Along the way, the crew became unhappy and **mutinied**. Another ship deserted the journey. Three ships continued. They sailed through a **strait** that led to a surprise—the Pacific Ocean.

Only one of Magellan's ships made it around the world and back to Spain. And Magellan was not on it. He died in battle in the Philippines and never reached the Spice Islands himself. But his expedition delivered information back to Europe. Europeans learned of the Pacific Ocean. They learned more about Earth's true size. The Strait of Magellan was named in honor of the explorer.

Magellan's History

Magellan was Portuguese but the government would not fund his expedition to the Spice Islands. So, he moved to Spain. The grandson of the rulers who sponsored Columbus agreed to support Magellan.

Ferdinand Magellan

Who Will Rule the World?

As the years went on, Spain and Portugal continued their **rivalry**. They raced to explore the world. They competed to claim new territory and to control trade.

Yet Spain and Portugal were not the only countries to recognize the value of trade and exploration. During the Age of Discovery, other European countries were also interested in exploring the world. They, too, wanted to trade for goods and wealth. They wanted to claim new land. In the 16th century, these countries stepped up their efforts, and more explorers took to the seas. They sailed for France, England, and the Dutch of the Netherlands.

Trade was one reason Europeans wanted to reach new lands. Religion was another. Europeans were Christians. American Indians were not. Europeans believed it was their duty to **convert** American Indians. They wanted to spread their beliefs. This was part of the reason these countries joined the race to explore.

American Indians bring furs to trade with the Dutch in the 1600s.

England

Netherlands

Portugal

France

Spain

Missionaries try to convert American Indians.

France also wanted to sail west. But the country needed explorers. Giovanni da Verrazzano was eager to help. He sailed to the New World for France in the 1520s. He was tasked with finding a route to India. He did not find it. But he did bring back more information about North America's east coast.

Jacques Cartier (ZHAHK CAR-tee-ay) sailed for France in 1534. He also set out to find a water route to Asia. He didn't find it either. He claimed territory in Canada for France. But the king was disappointed. Cartier made enemies in the New World. And he failed to find gold and diamonds. France lost interest in exploration for more than half a century.

The English picked up where France left off. Martin Frobisher went looking for a passage to Asia in the late 16th century. He also hoped to find treasure in North America. He found neither. Instead, he explored Canada for England.

Francis Drake led an expedition for England in 1577. He sailed through the Strait of Magellan. He claimed what is known today as California for England. When he returned, he was knighted. It was a huge honor. He was the first English explorer to **circumnavigate** the globe.

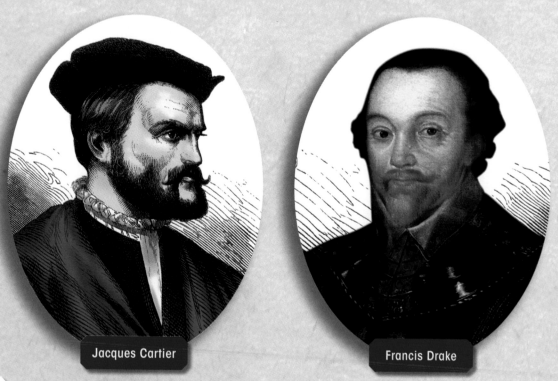

Jacques Cartier

Francis Drake

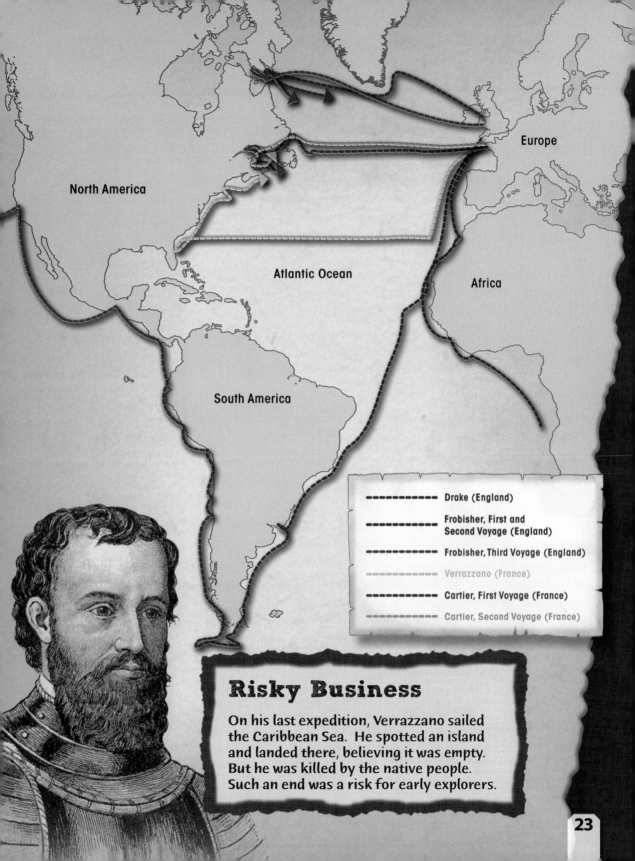

North America

Europe

Atlantic Ocean

Africa

South America

-------------	Drake (England)
-------------	Frobisher, First and Second Voyage (England)
-------------	Frobisher, Third Voyage (England)
-------------	Verrazzano (France)
-------------	Cartier, First Voyage (France)
-------------	Cartier, Second Voyage (France)

Risky Business

On his last expedition, Verrazzano sailed the Caribbean Sea. He spotted an island and landed there, believing it was empty. But he was killed by the native people. Such an end was a risk for early explorers.

In 1607, the Muscovy Company of London hired Henry Hudson as an explorer. He believed he could find a quicker passage to Asia through the Arctic Ocean. It was an icy passage. Two voyages failed when he had to turn back.

England lost confidence in him, but Hudson was determined to sail again. On his third expedition, he sailed for the Dutch East India Company. When ice blocked his path, he went to North America instead. There, he sailed on a river later named in his honor.

coin used by the Dutch East India Company

The Dutch East India Company

The Dutch East India Company was founded in 1602. It helped the Dutch gain independence from Spain. It led exploration efforts for the Dutch. It also protected Dutch trade interests. The company dissolved in 1799.

Henry Hudson lands in New York in 1609.

On his last expedition, Hudson once again sailed to the Arctic Ocean for England. He came across a bay that would later be named Hudson Bay. But soon, his ship was trapped in ice. He and his crew had to spend the winter there. Food supplies ran low. Hudson's crew suspected he was hoarding food to share with his favorite crew members.

By June, the ice melted and the ship could finally sail home. But harsh weather conditions and stormy seas were not the only dangers early explorers faced. Hudson's own crew was his undoing. Starving and angry, the crew forced Hudson off the ship onto a small boat with a few other men. They were never heard from again.

New Technology

New technology made navigation easier for explorers in the late 16th century. The back staff was invented in 1594. Like the cross-staff, it was used to measure distance north of the **equator**. It took measurements between the horizon and the sun's shadow.

back staff

Changing the World

Early explorers did not know much about the world. They did not know where the waters would lead them. They didn't always know when they would find land. And they did not know whether they would find people in these new places. Explorers ventured into the unknown with few tools to navigate. Some craved adventure. Others wanted fame and fortune. All of them set out with hope, and they risked their lives for their missions. They didn't know whether they would return to their homelands again.

world map from 1321

Vikings

The early explorers did not always find what they were looking for, but even unsuccessful voyages led to new knowledge about the **geography** of the world. They began trading with people in the New World. This would later lead to European settlements there.

Their expeditions did not always end well. The nations for which they worked believed they had a right to claim any land and take any resources they could by force. But for good or for bad, these explorers are now a part of history. They helped create the world we know today.

Amerigo Vespucci

Christopher Columbus

Ferdinand Magellan

Map It!

Early explorers mapped the globe. They set out with simple tools, and they made and improved maps.

Imagine you are a European explorer. You have just landed on an unmapped island in the New World. Draw a map of the island. Write notes about what you see. Then, write a letter to your family in Europe explaining your experiences. Include details about the journey and the new land that you are exploring. Explain to your family why your expedition is important.

Glossary

ambitious—having a desire to be successful, powerful, or famous

circumnavigate—to travel all the way around something

continents—the seven large land masses of Earth

convert—to change from one religion or belief to another

credited—gave honor or special attention to someone for an accomplishment

cultures—the beliefs and ways of groups of people

customs—traditional behaviors or actions of a group of people

empires—groups of countries that are controlled by one ruler

equator—an imaginary circle around the middle of Earth that is the same distance from the North Pole and the South Pole

expeditions—journeys led by people for a specific purpose

fleet—a group of ships that work together

geography—the natural features, such as rivers and mountains, of a place

horizon—the line where the land or sea seems to meet the sky

mutinied—a situation in which sailors refused to take orders and tried to take control from their commander

native—a person from a group of people who were living in an area when Europeans first arrived

rivalry—a situation in which people are competing with each other

sponsor—to pay for an activity or event

strait—a narrow passage of water that connects two larger bodies of water

treaty—an official agreement made between two or more countries or groups

Index

World Geography

This map is from 1321. Study it closely. Then, find a map from today. Compare and contrast the two maps and record your findings. How might early ideas about geography have influenced explorers' travels? How might this have made exploration difficult? Discuss these ideas with a friend or family member.